concentricity

Sheila E. Murphy

CONCENTRICITY

PLEASURE BOAT STUDIO:
A LITERARY PRESS

The author wishes to thank the editors of the following
publications in which current or earlier versions of
some of these poems first appeared:

*Asylums & Labyrinths; Key Satch(el); Brass City Review;
Rampike; The Lummox Journal; Po'Fly; Syntactics; N/Yes;
Yefief; Displace; Prosodia; Neologisms; Unicorn; Mesechabe;
Columbia Poetry Review; Misc. Proj.; Sycamore Review;
First Offense; Veer; Split Shift; Kings Estate Press;
The Screaming Ray Review; Gestalten; Pig Iron; Juxta*

ISBN: 1-929355-16-5

First Printing

Library of Congress Control Number: 2003112886

Cover Art: copyright © 2003 by Sheila E. Murphy

Book Design: JB Bryan

Set in Janson

Author Photograph: copyright © 2002 by Beverly Carver

Printed in USA

Published by Pleasure Boat Studio: A Literary Press
201 W. 89th Street, #6F
New York, NY 10024

Contents

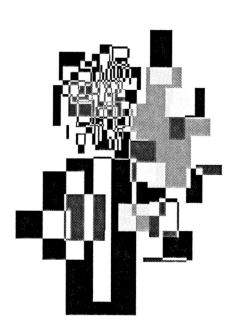

Of Lullaby

My orchids suffer from your paramilitary attitude. Won't
you touch me? Every bit of lullaby soothes moments of the
hurt, despite the uniform and lovely water. What is known
of our biographies: that they belong to us and fan out into
meanings. Cuff links rubbed to a dramatic shine. Pristine
things swerve into relationship with seasoned elements.
Can a habit be unlearned? A white shirt used to clean unruly
appliances. Real flowers in the photograph appear afford-
able. Phases of our joining include partial poverty. Would
seem refreshing as respect. As familiar as the word *tulip*
where the flower has been unframed petal flesh. The desire
to pulp a value. Quantify the fact of touch as hospitality. To
temper parchment with pressed flower skin held in a book.

Faculty of memory, the way you looked, and still the earth
around these other tangibles

A Limited Edition Lust

How do you reciprocate the act of smothering? Control
spawns jewelry made from breath's rubbing the mirror
clean and dry. One looks peaceful, while the other peeks out
from behind a clumsy shadow in pursuit of independence.
*I watched the penmanship begin to falter into age that he could
not resemble perfectly.* A gentleman stepped from the shower
with a pensiveness less sharable than certain. Misting some
of the occasion. No one certain who he was. Few write
letters anymore, much less love tunes that flow from left to
right on five-lined sheets. The fabric strays from clarity to
something sweet to touch as this companionship. A limited
edition lust shifts conversation from a breezeway to a bold
alert for rationing. Most of the men considered themselves
heat lamps. Most of the women did not seek the sun. Who
does not seem interesting beside a crowd of strangers?
Someone truly interesting.

Elusive Paycheck

I am not a cinder. Do you blank me? What shaped mirror
do I hold to you? Am diamond refund. Back to square. Am
longing, lofty doctrinaire. Am long on bonds and short on
coin. The squall will parse things as amendments to the
lofty sitcoms. *Are you there?* The mozzarella leans in close.
Restricts me to the gooseneck shaped like myriad filmed
silvers. When will the ever promised mist come home to
page? Never will get used to an elusive paycheck. Commas
plunked down like collateral sing ominosity of postpone-
ment set to music. Will there ever be a *there* to poke fun at?
My silence is presumed a symptom. I attract. For instance
I can neptune clear across the hall. Perambulators glisten
when presented to the swell guy learning on the banister. It
used to be like peristalsis here and now it's turned to crumbs.

Template, forms of unison, shelter as withdrawal

Fraypoints

Leaves green themselves past budding. Tea malt codifies
hegemony. And when we're slow, we're sampled in paren-
theses. The symbolism leaks fraypoints when we smother
our cadavers home. Come close and water me. If I were
seventy, I'd need a crane to move my books. I would avoid
stilts and sip with confidence stability, panache. Near the ivy
is more ivy. Near the strains of numinous vibrato I confront
the real output of scars. Primacy recency adopts new flavor
and delivers lumbar, texture, plenitude. How many ounces
are we dancing in (dependently)? The new birds squall as
they are formed. We're finding more of our declensions.
Raw, from scratch, out-of-the-box the way we do, and all at
once as children with blueberry mindsets all our own.

Dislikes

Dyslex, I thought he'd said. No shadow is worth being
salted. His eternal *award,* my father stressed. Mid-course
corrections seem like lobs over a short fence. Wheat grass in
tiny quantities enhances *what?* Embarrassment surrounds
the words *a little slow.* People laugh nervously on hearing
the addendum *mental. Tough* becomes the next word.
Distinct from Golden Mean. Are there things we can laugh
off? The idea is to cease and reconfigure tepid nonchalance.
The luck. And *chercher* (en francais) the room where we
were wed then several sentences beyond the several sylls- as
mussed as cabaret. Lengthwise the temperature mid-
sectioning these white alert first blues tempura altogether
rapt and such. The omniture. The look and feel, the sound
of . . .

Vault

We have bootlegged matching body chemistries. I hear this is a suites hotel where each one's neck and neck with strangers capable of Rolfing or deciphering Egyptian characters. The lapdog of our sensibilities calms strangers. Equally, viscosity deranges pulp and garden tools and heavy-armed equipment. She said that he reminded her of slim pond prose. She was wearing six-plus pounds of tone. Levels impulsed their way to my cravat. I simply soloed out of reach and madcap heresy just out of strict conformance. It takes several spare monks to jumpstart a religion. Several under-recognized hewn minds. Cane sugar in sufficient quantity to unseam the emotions cantilevered in teased tragedies.

Concentricity

Installations house imaginary stallions. *I dreamed erasure of oncoming achievement*, shared thus shelved. The episode was focused on how I might say no to kin requests. The harm seemed morphine as dishonesty painted experience a cool blue. A woman to whom I'd handed my whole personality returned from the performance to alert me to simplicity. I am acquainted with this brand of hiding. People do not lean out from their beds to answer accusations, invitations, halves of hypothetical debate. All ponds appear the same to me. All anaerobic exercise seems desk time. Voluntary trapeze artistry adopted chivalry as first disguise. Historians in my experience don't gravitate toward convertibles. Rest stops dot the landscape. One of the two, en route to a funeral, plotted the likely stops. Black birds tasted sky in unison. Her eyes when closed were just as lovely, riding. She smoked gently a cigarette between hums. Obligations broke off into slogans to eradicate a feathery falsetto. Curiosity and respiration aren't the same. *Amateur* of course refers to the air quality. Small temple's ice changing its chemistry to water running down the stained glass windows.

The Sorting Process

She said evidence of craft within a person had its edges. She said color of the tight vest ought to be some kind of a criterion but that would never likely fly. I wondered for a moment about credibility I had all along assigned to her. I wondered how derivative I might be, standing on wet pavement, trying to construct some permaculture from the spatty pools and shiny leaves and soggy things once thrown away. What constitutes success? The way the papers read and tanned announcers have it, you would think that a prerequisite was a fleeting nature linked with imprecision. I don't mean to suggest I see a problem. Whatever rigor we can muster is as good as what uneducated people had after exposure to great minds that placed in cupboards various ideas that served several people's purposes long enough to stick. Even ardent prejudice has sold well and continues to, depending on positioning. Depending also on competing headlines, and what has won the coveted attention space of fifteen seconds, during which the listeners tell themselves they are committed to this learning and will follow through of course with lives that prove their good intentions.

The Finish Line

There was this blueline master you would *drill* for. It just *hugged* the episodic part of me, kept waiting in the ruminative patch of antlers. Seized with (shall I call it) *rhapsody* you could construct yourself by lining up the endpoints. At least that's how I think of them, as roads through places they were going to. And that's the finish line that spells abandonment they're all discussing epidemically. I remember mooseheads in the doctor's anteroom in Mishawaka. It was dark in there; you could imagine viral intercourse outside the antiseptic sanctum where the smell of alcohol on cotton balls seemed linked to throat sticks. The doctor's manner cuffed you in a way with stylistic health that might preclude him. I would leaf through magazines that left no space for thinking and continue making lines touch, mazing up the place with fully webbed thought. Consequences factor in ahead of time if you're the sort of person who uncoats the little lambskin of a walk toward destiny. We're stuffed with intervention and with self-control. When is body posture going to leave its calcium deposits on another person's mood. There are already ones of us who sweep up matter like new fools. As though positioned in a club that half includes the seedlings of credentials substituting for live souls. *Just mesh with something* goes the cant. Just press your velvet lines on top of evolution and imagine. *Close your eyes.* The stop watch never has to glow. We're principled as haste and tender offers crave attention from us. I resolved to have released prior vocabulary, suspecting it would alter my demeanor from example to exemplum. No such taste. It's each sense for itself, not tied explicitly to gender. What protons want, protons acquire. You (all of you) are free to document the headers and the footers and the contents. Fire and glaze and seaside your way past the menagerie upon menage. It's quiet in more places than Antarctica, especially if you're committed to pronouncing all its consonants.

Temp

Each day's a dozen more unlike it. Sentences might be from anyone. Wood carving settled dust of onomatopoeia once, a hundred times. One false mood and ridicule becomes the currency of favor. Hedging grows into a specialty. The numb safe drone of repetition lulls her spirit back to sleep. A learning curve as shapely as her expectation of it flings against against wallspace, one thought at a time. She logjams her way back to reflexes rumored to be natural. A cold knell chastens vertebrae one at a time listless or driven by appearance posing as reality. She pinches strong clamps from the time clock and begins as a chameleon unwittingly assists in the resurfacing of scenery. She propels the singing voices into play absent a tuning fork reputed to be true.

Simplicity That Stretches

Mythology refuses to go forth and multiply a cinder or cold
jewel. Heart's argument becomes an indefatigable simplicity
that stretches only when stretched to. Omnivores implant
the feel of pantomime to be polite. The blank check we
thought we knew was coated with a parlor game of keep
away. Her least known painting called "Still Shot with
Shoulders," remained dangerously near the spine. And
blinds sang shut the moment that she drew the cord.

Sweet Crescendo Pie

I like my gender opal when it's stuck so we can ridicule our
settlers as the antelope they play. Rude mire cusps a new
house riddle to my tonguing. The truckload of unwanted
things can make me spiel all over whiteboards information
I've made up. To fill timetables given till I'm ripe enough to
fall into unspongy land foretasted, wrung. The waspy little
henchman suckles bric-a-brac as curvy little ice pings center
weeds in the untaunted west. Do chemists have to own
excuses for their limp white shelves bereft of stock? Why am
I stuttering the answers to another quiz? It's two-ply ring
toss once again and, buster, these, our children, have to soap
somebody's window to get home. It's in their craw unwanted
so fresh paint to be gainsharing wood looking munificence.
Come wildly to the forefront home bedraggle me just south
of where a birthpoint shall be spoken till a burial. When
comfort asks a little sewing, lower shades until the season
shifts. Then be nude and slander any pie place happened as
the justice system musses driveways with our symbols of the
range parked in.

Lastingly, the houseprints scent open a ready stratosphere in
welcome of the spruce lank wisps of rain

The Solo of Detail

He lived beside a megaphone that made food purchases, balanced checks, prevented loneliness. Then all tone matching ceased. How simple, when a thing is over, to refashion it. Quiet seemed a viable, long-term solution to the years of being loved in that conspicuous full way that prompts a form of rage no one can understand. He liked his soft bright clothes. He liked being a fraction of some fruitful thing. Church was an easy system to keep rote. You used certain nouns and made the reverend think his trend was catching on. Until today, too little had been thought through. Which grew blatant in the absence of that sound, thereby highlighting all preached syllables. Through the filter of an absent hearing aid he used to hide unwanted words that passed for a presumed affection. He saw himself in patches of the unkempt land that seemed to need no wind. He tried to like what he had known and what he was until the noise of people thumbed its way into his ken again. The preacher's decibels, the neighbors, and refrains that came back into all memory's elastic temperature. The gloss of being by himself, all a memento. Piece by piece he learned himself again in quiet with just birds alongside home without companionship. The solo of detail.

A Change in all the Breathing

Cement meshes with symptoms. Just as thought quintuples phobias the same as mercy kill. Sweet wood offloads intact notes to draft. A semblance of the same small politics of statutes. Midriff pieced together halfway thrives. This close to death, a change in all the breathing. Wood inserts details after commodities. The situation ethics log on to a hundred likely smiles. At snailspeed, very few are scenery to hold. Some crescent rolls precede the tension in a quake to vacillate between symptoms and wash. The first semester sanctifies by rote the cortisone. Entirely episcopal with desert flute. One kind of wood. A hundred trees distracting.

Foreplay

Mirage quintuples facelift catalogues so smoothly, any fossil
would divulge a secret past of quorum specified by four-
laned highways. Snap sugar peas equip the reasoning power
of craft. The sum total of constraints is policy. A velvet bow
around whatever gift was to be given back. Thumbs criticize
a motion visible. Community means sharing ovens that
make bread. As passing newly warmed bread hands receive,
accept. And shoulders demonstrate the strength to hold
what comes, toss of the die. A pretax vigil soaped with power
to renege and brash chance happenings. Is crime identical to
an absence of accountability? Calendula high fives annuncia-
tions past. The clumsy life force sans ingredients we labor to
demystify rings home barbells, cowbells, church bells.
Sandwich in the little dumpling adversarial arrangements.
Youth crimes value curfews. Three can linger. Four can fall
from space nets safe from their robust queues. Lasting
headrests give in to their limelight. Fractions caretake what
we've lost. Perhaps a late night coif. Surprise renditions of
patrols chemlab their way to health. Detached as dotted
Swiss but tough, resistant. Patience lets go leisure. Ritual
compress. So. As it was won and thought. Skill level
changes. Focus changes. What is reported shifts toward
wide end of the megaphone. Abrupt as civil court away from
comfort. Fear erased and often is. With morning an eternal
evidence.

Voice

A fingerprint attached itself to gut string and vibrated home
a little while. The consequence: attention talked into
significance. All eyes following, all ears, etcetera. Is it better
to have fresh cut flowers for the luncheon or brown betty
for dessert? The thing I most liked of her home was mea-
sured rest she counted palpably. When my time was up,
I knew enough to leave. I saw this calmed her. Tone
matching comes hard to would-be loved ones. At least we'd
conquered easily enough the challenge of hearing the same
tune. In unison seeking repeat signs. Most of water that
protects her home bears no relationship to thirst. Her ego
quenches other egos. Whatever protocol grows feverish
is right when it's prolonged. She offered easily her hand
I touched. On joining the string section, not the same as
concert mistress. Not alert with freeze frame duty. Never to
replace a son.

The Creases in Her Jigsaw

Human temperature went down a few degrees. Leaves changed paint. He simmered this and that clear broth. Iodine convinces. Crevices just past their prime have laminated scuffed and sugared templates. One of the full moons committed to memory unfaithfully dresses for meals. The creases in her jigsaw melded into reasons for a fractured picture. Who cares if you're famous. I am not appalling. Centuries will fail like bills to pass. A spouse is not a guarantee you'll like the odds. Sworn officers conform to mettle pre-determined. Cost of doing business returns serve. Snips the life from corners. Butterflies are not connected to unpleasantness. Miraculous new forms of fun appeal. Do betters lengthen their careers. How little is required to add a plus or minus to one life.

Heart

She wears wool soulfully (and yet) the singing hilltops ask
amendments only of themselves. The carnivores are every-
thing but plastic. If you can imagine harboring impatience,
you are aware how little playthings get to mimic shelves.
Circumference is back in fashion. Pit bulls naturally ignite.
The pilgrims really owned no semblance of religion. (Have
I mentioned carnivores). Cement blocks roam these fields.
And who among us naturally forecasts pigment, sequins,
light. The phosphorus is bittersweet. The chemlab salts its
way back home. Even roads wore clean perfume of an
escape. Vermillion bases blue unguessed. To hammer is to
give back sainthood. Shores of lake are back in fashion. Pies
along the green smooth lake emit the kinds of chemicals to
be back into, following *away from*. Sandwiches unziplock
sleeves that form exteriors. Platforms have us on them.
Panting distracts from anything occurring. Safety and
distance, too much alike to be alike (for good). The raging
heat. The purpose of a club. Or saddle sores. Wheels
don't often find themselves. Most used nouns syndicate
their pretty dress. A violation patterned after glacier parks
precede autobiographies. With change so close . . . a
milestone peaks toward points of suffrage. Arms usually
positioned, traced.

Anatomy

Some forearms lack relinquity. An almost palpable resistance
to new starts blocks figurative arteries that route pulsehood
rumored to be needed. Some players do not care about
advancing strangers via once-removed accomplishments.
Give back remains a mythical dissemblance. Citizens who've
worked their lives into a stupor modify an unexpected word,
a phrase, form catch-all correspondence. Magnifying grace
eclipses plain and solid objects at a certain time of night.
Coffers with welts on them resume their good luck stance
until the right people arrive. Soprano hesitation's not the
norm. Perplexity redeems the acre of its scorch, awaiting the
right time. Fashionable quarantine denotes a monster of
disease deprived of freedom. Metronomed as we all are to
voices that mince zilch close to the holidays. Weariness
would exercise its bluing capability so collars lose no starch
and bodies just assigned to them stay crisp. The heaven of it
all recedes into a background sound accused of being coy
but not unmuscled.

Heraclitus Once / Again

Merle Adams. Merle Adams. Please pick up a white paging phone. Resilience half-contagious illustrates that ring toss knows no reciprocity. Once thumbs-down is given, what can be toast? Memoranda clutch their makers. It is noon. I time my getting spacefully. This curious ecclesiastical refreshment snow for better in my purse. Windflow entreats what you are watching is the same as what you are. One carnivore retreats. *Rhinoceros.* Sequentially the tapers yawn themselves from peak to slope, whose ribbon lacks a little twist. C-clamps are only slightly toned. In fever, I hear blanket between fingers louden so it's never lonely and unquiet. Footnotes are lighter fluid. Doesn't wool feel kind to skin? Cylindrical compartments transport money through a glass tube via vacuum. If you want a back that you can count on, quit sitting on your change.

Selfish

Someone squeezed her purse once until out jumped
wealth without its casing. There she stood humiliated by
the neighbors' view in their binoculars of empty tweed, the
gilded butterflies of life-sized diary pages. Now she wears
a periscope taped to her eye. She checks the view of every-
where and not politely anymore. She cross checks possible
mistakes as probable as tiresome winter. Within reach of
cold still close to how it feels when friends' affections wither.
Cough prints not contagious catch the forelight within sky.
How do you get in front of anything you'd ask yourself?
Gather as in idleness the courage to kick into an overdrive
component that relates to scarcity in pure crystal form.
Pretty much the first thing to go is the cash followed by
simmered sheets and watch fob. Please explain.

Course correct, a splash of brandy, trust in hand

Priest Kiss Every Likely Loveliness

If pagination once precludes the printing function, some
of what is left within my heart won't suffocate an object of
affection. Sacrifice whomever we are willing to relate.
Naivete once presented as a prize combs the remaining
afghan. Sports retain their semblance to hypocrisy. It all
looks good by morning once you've larked enough to count
your spurs and creases. Penury was never soft as angles to
the north inclusive of known benchmarks. Megahertz is
singular adjustment of the play in work, printing the desire
points in a softest blue. Once saturation grands its languor
we would priest kiss every likely loveliness. Charmed
exception saves us home. An attitude sums practice till we
learn to want it. Can you help, yep, you betcha. Do we
bury what we love? Do courses really crash when faced
with favorites to be played. A modular approach much like
an auto body at the canyon's base comes home. My first
question: did you *read* the document, and if not why not?
Shifts apply to more than shapeliness. Sources of funding
crispen what we want. Peak workload outside her expertise.
The rich ones show themselves to be low-flying planes.
A certain sizzle tames when subdivided into quantities.
Proactive lice afford the heads they land on. Sacristies are
rarely plural. Differentiate between refinement and finesse.
Discord reveals itself to be without thorns where the mildest
roses *punge*. The wildest philosophical appliances seem

drugged to the untrained eye. May I often romp with you apart from work that you love most? To be apart occurs and to be worldly open to suggestion. Reinforce policies that make occur what will. With seasoning and intricate receptions. So we accept unprioritized accomplishments.

Reunion

Our little present tense was thatched. It seemed the lack
of medication trespassed on a quid pro quo. The lasso
thumbed its way due west. She shallowed the on-top-of
cure. Each one of us fed lumber to the lapping plan of fire.
If someone measured quickness of the flicker in our sight.
Rack and pinion sanctifies. The place beneath her eyelids
felt unsure. It all was warm again. And twenty-three years
melted with the lack of rain. Narration basked in hindsight.
Trends changed without speech and after. To resume was
inefficient. Singe quickens thirst still unrecorded landfill.
In the place where limits are, we taste. Then think
through many times. Green yarn in flame. Not one of
us a true soprano.

Cartography

Cartography trims beards a little bit. Demographers
melt down snub-nosed weapons not because of loneliness.
Simple battalions confiscate one drug after the next. Who
has the guts to trace a wounded body just to clarify? For
doppelgangers burn up fuel much like the rest of us. So
what if exit's symptomatic of aggressive maladjustment
therapy. The one white rose remains too long-stemmed for
our horizontion. I recall the judge's quipping that the wrong
group had been sued. In the case before him the defense was
being held hostage by spousal cravings for abuse. Mythical
families brought mythical comfort. She wrote a memo to
her children that they must not rage. The one who could
read vetoed her plan, and soon antique eggs smashed,
released the smell of sulfur all throughout the house. I've
often wondered, would the therapist be likable outside those
safe, beige walls. She has a look that I interpret to mean all
cylinders have fired. The small umbrellas that defined each
separate meeting at the bagel shop also disguised intensity.
To have once deciphered and interpreted to mean a round
of clear emotion. Care packages allowed to spill over into
unmet needs carried by rumor into windmills sketched by
hand on napkins with the earthtone logo on.

Jazz 'Versation

Cadenzas do the blushing for us. Jazz 'versation isn't quite
reflexive. Tote that Marge voice out of the Gillespie frame.
Before most references pass they offer an impression this
all's an imprecise sort of a music farm. Distance lacking the
routine fever practicum says everything's the same. *Who'd
know a wrong note in a foreign language?* In which all speakers
look the same. But that isn't why we're here today. We're
here to consecrate a prophet whose energy has piled up for
so long we forgot to recognize . . . And Hershey-flavored
half adagio resembles giddiness refined to such a pitch that it
sounds perfect on first take. Yielding a proof sheet with a
single shot repleting every wallet on the set. That leads us all
to seem alike as premised more than once. While pulling
away from gravity's bear market of a hug.

Freight

Concomitant neglect sings in the bake sale choir.
Immodest amounts are given to those proclaiming quiet
lives. Identified enlistments leave church speakers usually
in voice. Coined language lands in boxcars hollowed out
of symptoms cozily undressed. One feather at a time
delinquent in response to the longevity. Always striving
to press weight in excess of one's own. Helmet preventing
the oncoming obstacles. A primavera impulse flanking
quarterbacks and prima b's. All costumed inside weather
in their prime. Soon rinsed by shared palaver rumored to
be ashes holding weights in tow. As rumination passes
wealth, peace, headlines. Commas on the page and breath
accompanying.

Practicum

Soprano Volvos peer-assess a myriad of flavors patently
aligned due north. Familiar scoreboards shame pyrotechnics
into comfort zones like same-sex wheat while in-house
histrionics rise into the zone of happy bread. Who wants
to catalogue an acquiescive sundown? Postures recoup
brands willflowering the venture backers lanky as rescinded
text. Speech recognition curtsies to the penetration of
touch-tone. Automation likes to blossom hobbies close to
practice of undress. The visor plays with eyesight as opposed
to center stage. The escalator plummets till we're free of
debt. Connectedness repeals known leverage. Most of the
secretions plan to quake when anyone's no longer looking.
Tools make gray tones rasp the way familiar consonants
emit a singsong light including meaning. Bushels of new
crop curve to the fibrillating left. Why not old-fashioned
confidence? Why not aversion to neglect? The pomegran-
ate seeds taste candied crashing down on fundamentals.
Nordic windows let go nests of dollars close to inner circle
hearts. Remarks fall to the kindred floor in quantities well
known. Familiar syntax frames what we economize during
the inabundant downtime larky as a mobile looking tentative
in wind.

Forty-Five Or So

I was working half forever, unaccustomed to a chaos
rumored to be seminal. No wonder birth is tepid before
clumsing true. On TV at the gym, the face of Flynt, the
face of Jong. I could not read the underwords. Kept
pumping muscles gone a little flat. The language I might
use for the stenographer has no context in a ripe new
sphere. Also, the meaning that I might infer would not be
blight unless I'm trembly twice as much as ferment would
allow. Nine twenty-four, and all that I can think is when
I crawled back into bed after shuttling guests to meet a
pre-dawn flight. The hand that smoothed across my back
and tailbone is asleep. Unleashes every spontaneity I stay
too young to recommend. The feast accommodates me
glandly. Where are fragrant recollections when we try not
to impound them? Furnaces might come in blue, but no
one asks repeatedly.

Some birthday candles thrown together randomly, purse
fully accounted for, a sip of ginseng tea

And She Was Losing Hair

She had an almanac on her bookshelf, and since I did not
know her yet, I scanned what else was there. She also
had a photograph of two small boys. And she was losing
hair. The books that she used most looked unreliable,
homemade. I paid for her experience and its sprawl across
presumably like situations. Mountains held us at a distance
still polite. We sat remotely in their arms having in common
more than we would learn until the fates kissed something
they should kiss. And we'd acknowledge that. The clocks
would genuflect to compasses and we'd move on with lives
we leased like pretty cars to be released when hammering
out details. Finances are a subset of democracy, itself a
subset of the long solo performances that ultimately appear
to clash. But that is just one version of the blues.

Simplicity That Stretches

Mythology refuses to go forth and multiply a cinder or cold jewel. Heart's argument becomes an indefatigable simplicity that stretches only when stretched to. Omnivores implant the feel of pantomime to be contrite. The blank check we thought we knew was coated with a parlor game of keep away. Her least known painting called "Still Shot with Shoulders" remained dangerously beside the spine. And blinds sang shut the moment that she drew the cord.

Her Body

What do snails of any gender matter? The evening of a
birthday, balancing her checkbook, listening to the tele-
phone wedge love between the usualities. Consume,
perspire, give thanks. Mute button a screen saver for the
soul. It is a smooth and qualmless afternoon all lifetime.
Forty-five today and capable of not painting thought.
Speaks while regarding programmed scenes. She starts
to love her instrument with fervor. To anticipate precisely
no return as an expenditure of energy. Her body easily
perspires life processes she would release as naturally as
childhood. A relationship is sitting together, partially
approaching unknown subjects. Refraining from talk that
has no need. So is transcended by a comfort level. Seashells
collected placed on wreaths. Capacity to watch something
and not say. As though agreed upon. Though nothing is.
As saints go on being acknowledged, attentive minds
enforce a certain lack of ego in those holy ones whose
hands have the capacity to heal. Who leave not one mood
frightened, faltering.

Protection

Rhumba, samba, doe-eyed opposite of clash is education.
Pens to match the theobald of summer slingshot into
monster's eye. Spotted on the cry end of a seamed chaise
facing all the brick light of a world through olive palms
and chaps on someone riding. Do the half tones rise with
Adam's apple to the sonnet in a copybook? And do the
whiled appointments harbor space of modesty? Cold bristles
soften to the lanolin-bathed fingers close to sheep in
lengths of semi-automatic light. A gathering of leathergold
still suitable for taming. Learning light resides in factual
compendia of common names empropered toward a sense
uncommon where shoelaces meet the shadescape sequenced
here among the sleight of broomlight

Chance as a religion popeless in economy

Midriff

Fullness doubles over in flight training school. Imposture kindles something even stationery cannot soothe. In film footage we view acres of hats. Arm motions that look brittle in their emphasis. Quirks of the very fate we have induced by virtue of our craft or lack thereof. Pair of glasses to repeal inaccurate long life. The actuality is fluted graveside. Two small flowers no different from a multi-paned glass building shepherding the eccentricities. Poured on them as all life forms. A pale quiet comes over the absence of imagination where a fundamental lapse is heard. No matter how long preparation and commitment last, the body will be rinsed. Responsiveness accepts without excessive phosphate. Fish touch crowded corners all irate and trembling. Caught simple as sky's breath comatose or bleating. Chamomile's smooth steam to open one after the next detail.

In Motion

Gentian violet sounds Elizabethan when you've lived your whole life in a room in front of something capable of going on without you. Traction isn't meant to freighten. The worst form of collapse is nervous, makes me thus. *En route to Tucson, he left me the expected voice mail saying that he loves me and is on his way.* I am especially suited to being a love object to people in the state of flux. In motion, I compose. The video of famous train rides emphasizing Canada unleashed a fantasy. In the sleeper car, a man was in his pull-down bed reading *The Globe and Mail* as his own train sped past ingenious scenery. The privacy of motion intersected with concurrency that would persuade you marzipan is always being made somewhere. The monks in chorus out my CD speaker holes are praying now, and that is why we still exist.

The Sacrament of One Small Note

She calls me away from my own absolution to hear the
smatter bird rehearse an inkling of the single note absorbed
from a parental mockingbird. The telephone interrupts with
just a slice of business well negotiated that could lead to
other helpings. My theory has been and continues to
develop cumulative truth. As if and only if. We prefer
absorption of the carpet once called *wall-to-wall*. I press my
ear against the heavy door aslant on hinges to hear the
sacrament of one small note. My life in segments, strands,
amid capacity learned just in time to weave them.

Matches

Matches not so plentiful now that the three smokers left, are
standing in the yard like some small social club before the
population rose. What do they talk about besides the
singularity of smoke? The pigeons near the capital also leave
a residue. Air in this one corner is less sweet. People look
out windows to adore the trees, and one sliver of recall
when each thing was tentative. People who are not outside
wish they could be outside. The only ones who qualify are
those able to spoil the atmosphere while feigning innocence
about it all. That said, I treasure smoke smell, even from
cigarettes. I still feel the trickle of what was sexy and
desirable in film, those hats that frame deceptive eyes.
The cool exhale is actually a hot. Associations of a whistle
pearl the aftermath of something intimate of short duration.

Evidence, itself ephemeral, that a painter might include
within the work

The Meta-Ecstasy Sells Short

Each subtraction first convinces that tradition's a baton. That fig leaf over deals not what they used to be. Throngs' recollection. A temerity goes father-limp. Men in the dream thick with repair. The state of dis-. Sunbathing in the very much unglued soft water. Rebels leaven in wall sockets where some spaces in between allow the luxury of eccentricity. Grant unto them (Lord) a potent reciprocity. Mention rotundity and then some fuss extraneous. Calendula returns lightly the serve. Fast forward taxes bags under the eyes. The meta-ecstasy sells short day-old patina. Some pink in it so far. Forelockable as seat belts. She rubbed the sitcom so oblivion first faltered on two wheels. The ultimately selfish guest erased a continent depicted pale eye blue. At center table was a glass bowl to replace the trapezoid. Whose deadline was intentionally missed?

The Trills (Ninefold)

Precipitous aplomb mildews our dreamed indulgence. Was
there ever an economy? The trills (ninefold) demean the
licensure. More tract than fasting. Silence moans through
streetlamps quieting the blunt new hills. I hear a bird thus
confiscate peer meadows in the rugged press of thought
time. Sacrilege is so much mist. The avenues, I hear, have
mostly sequined modes of dress. Sufficient years go by to
trouble anyone with leisured offspring. As decision's one
form of direct address. Penurious attention spans the
module's wholesomeness. Collapsed new far-flung camisole
(unless). Perchance to drive away a few more fears. With
lunging in the distant past. Unmonied, one must dissipate
the shadows. Almost gray as slender host. The leanings and
the dry sheep worthy. Or the clear arrangement or the
sequiturs intact. Whenever promised road shows. Pomp and
gravy move in last. As timely as a weather roves (as grass).
The *de rigeur* of hastened flow. My last accounting. Rose
penitence and sure the lingering. Of snow. And were there
few or several more. The hate mail fastened to a post.

Inclement Ruse

Some sketches leave out text. Others minimize the fitted
doors. Four posters carve a space around the sleep's relay
of passing on. To have amply loved is serially rich.
Concomitance in breast pocket heavies suppositions of
our worth. Cement fails every time to rise. Handfuls of
grain repeal erasure. Opportunity's a hollow word. Some
squares where we might place them. Richness maintains
promises and curvy jumpropes housed at center field. The
yellow crops slow down in case of Hollywood. The mark
of a true friend is tendencies toward prime configuration.

My Son

Fertility makes me jibe with why I'm here. His intellect
invited mimicry. *My sacrifice* as planned by those with inside
information. We would make something of this loose nest
where a single twig has clout. The insufficient shoulders
of those governed as compared with his brawned fact.
Laws bluegreen gathered juice of the mature plants
needing to relax. *I am contextually no more than a pass-through
to succeeding generations.* With his watchful eye to guard me.
Habitat fulfilled. Excruciation plain and soldered. Not to
leave the house, excused on basis of potentiality. *When I show
picture frames, I show the monikers of youth also.* Wrest images
from all along the parkway most capriciously intact. Some
pots the source of argument. Whatever beauty is, it is in
pieces. Anymore, there's no worth in the sanguine. *Here
inside this frame intended to look good atop the piano is my son.
My Boniface.*

Lifeline Into

Etudes fail to go wild in the warm woods. Unplanted music
stands spread open into functionality at intervals. A hundred
nightfalls and a rousing canvas stretched to an intact, if
charitable, skin. Protection sinecured to left-right-left's own
pulchritude. Try bitters, echinacia, sown crops. Try sleep at
night, snipped corners, rotomontade. A lemon stand for
foolproof men with earning power studly as smooth-shaven
faces. Doubling is what incomes do amoebically. Assume
a value, spin the value, tweak a lifestyle, buy a Yorkie.
Blush your lifeline into crescent rolls, hotels, case-making
duplicates. Press here, there, in the penumbral quarters
much like loaves and creches. Dim the lights, prevaricate
with brothers you just met a mile from your last whim.
Exacerbate the crease in *spun*.

Home multiplied beyond its fallow soul until a mystery
affords requested triage

Sotto Voce Springtime

Turtle, butterfly, entire troops service local stitching of
connect points. Dotted mocha molecules and fresh ebbed
saints for patterned politics to soothe care in a packaged
diffidence. Mortuarial young cozies keep the tea abreast of
sotto voce spring time hazing much of a repeal away from
the distinction between grasp and faith. Their hedges
match the climax of an off-wing centimetric point free-
fallen on the yucca pains. We treetop and de-leave our
sudden children to the beaded quays of laciness. Old shoes
with tongues back in their heads backhand the salt from
Romanesque predominance. Apart from the stay singular
of an already jug-lit present to entire upon the gorgeous
name of William as it used to be.

Reading between syllables, true hearing, the formation
of decorum

A Slapstick Broth

I have decided to detail you to the back yard of intelligence
wield-y as a slapstick broth. When did you begin to listen
with your half swish of attention? I would domino your pack
point perfectly immersed in courage or vibrato. I would
round each corner not laying a patch. Our ceiling's still
undone. Your job becomes my curfew. The immodular
approach we share to greasepaint taxis to the shed where
we bane featherweight of slam dance in the bake sale of
imbalance. Forefront upon foe, the storage in my ship
shape clings to glory, and the mist slants toward unnoticed
soil. Give me a ballpoint of a quasi sail impromptu web
rind. With a kiln to give a lave as gastric as the tattles
and commercial cult. Be lilac when you seal the path to
repetition. I hear return of service qualms these streams
across.

Shipshape, doeskin, furnishings with garlic in the past

Unfocusing the Reason

You really are the perfect patient advocate, a good sport
about all this. Forget couplets. Full white pages, petals on a
fruit wink. Tap he has not done. A halting way of speaking.
Frock. Explain the drying after rain. Brick light. Seasoning
a taxicab unfocusing the reason all this happened. Prison
nouns along. "Not bad." The map of dotted swiss reversing
trespass. *Take me there.* Would suede help the relaxed fit.
Don't say French fray to a fine soft episode. Hair salted.
Reach me for. Lamps gone from here. Take avenues. I sit up
in hollyhock and call it bed. Call as I see . . . Affairs are for
arithmetic, no more. The average evangelist imbibing liquid
glyphed from some commercial feed. Where does each of
these small trinkets come from? Talk to the independent
English teachers of America. Tell them no one wastes
November, a mere prelude in the cotton fiber books. I look
to make a fortune then entirely relax into a likely form of
service.

Underscore what playthings do to what we were

Free-Poured

When applies to questions about sacredness. As *what* exhausts most nutrients. *Where* melts. *Why* lacks constitution. *Who* is too much variable. Seasoning takes long or not full walks across the register. I told you I would have to rearrange my mood if you persisted in this threat to add encumbrances. No single day is lost to lack of gratitude. It helps to write it down, whatever. *Careful where you walk.* The lawn's not what it was again. Function's drained from frolic if there ever was a bundle or a third bed. On vacation it is nice to sleep ahead. And get beyond the echoes. Fondly noted. And I think we have enough of everything to last a time. Why can't episodes be children? Quite impossibly awake again not worrying but sailing through the challenged looking weeds the symphonies the multiple credentials lolling in the baste way. Leave pratfalls to beg for real parts. Our future is in independent looking dominoes.

Free-pouring coffee lying in a mug caked with a kind of confidence

Ruse After

Installation makes me sick, or makes me think, I have
forgotten. Many parts of speech seem right to bear on
fatted calves that might be toothsome in someone's spare
time. Spare tires on fire are all the eaches we could want
and then some benefits, bananas, shot clocks. Who
ordered this sourpuss weather? I'm afraid of ostrich impulse
chronologically intact. Erasers on a chain around the neck
weigh something. Don't embarrass her with all the clatter
of enchantment focused on her prowess in keen living.
Ruse after ruse appends my living jitters. It is half the feast
of rain. Incentive presses on the corner lot and plants
belonging where we've combed them at least twice. If ever
any mourning dove were keen on mirror white, we would
transcend the half-mast thinking creviced where we'd
halfway smile. A potter's field is worn in our mean temperate
loom quiet. East of here the color violet sames the way our
weeks would be.

Chaperone of dances held amid the trees where boys live
with their duffel bags

The Weeds

Paralysis becomes the sword tap on a frightened shoulder.
When the body presses on a place that lamps the hand,
there is a cinder boiled too many times. Does the word
"Mishawaka" mean anything to you? Sleeves are victims
of a sequence that resembles stares. Too fraught with
conspicuous disjuncture ever to learn paint. The weeds
supposedly have virtue. Tame them, tame *me*. Edmonton,
Alberta is another place with raven-colored mother lodes
to try.

Her degree was from a wafer college basted the curriculum
parallels

Many Null Undressings

Longingly we have been multiplied adaptive. Then throngs
release (so tenderly) our others and with seven chimes
subtract what seems mid-earth. Command time falters in
the (all that I can think is) snow. The vector of my breath
influenced by slow-go. When we say *mercurial*, we've
tongued around the girly block so "awful" slow it's time to
turn the tidings print block north again. Our elders have
been fabe along the lines of any old mythology that we
can norm a little west of here. The sunny ones own cars.
They are our nurturants with stipples running breath joints.
Tell the others we have been *conceived of* and we count. Tell
midriff it is never taken further than our mal-connective
depth. So there you have the furry story. The Imelda-cide
and clatter of abstruse new wingspread lollies. Lamp me in
your width to maze the nearing toddy all the mink room
drastic powered day with daisies in the pipeline.

Gray Wood Gray

Meld me forth. I am convivial *entonces*. Ride share just a
little to the north. What is this endpoint play supposed to
summon in me? Pomp? Surpassing unenlightened rope
tricks that would dagger homeward. I have practiced
seeming not so young, but this is now. The stitches you
have left me in are firm and glad as sun-sprayed cleavage.
In the riptide park, I stand the grands and offer sofitel to
bargain beasts. There is a thirst one can't accommodate in
this much blue. Fly in tidy ointment now, the food, a half-
surprising tone of gray wood gray. The subjects left to talk
about the lamps without the frills. Are you tuned in to the
extent to which these folks are *slaves*? These personal details
cease to be interesting. As conscience starts to hoard the
pavement. . . Mardi Gras is sour by herself, feels she de-
serves a solo part inside the chorus of unhappiness. She
whines, no longer purrs. Her hormones are used car lots.
Pills she took have dried, and she refuses to make way for
mortal probabilities. Tedium's a draft. Here, fill this out,
reveal the all-too-human exhibition of a curve. Boxed-in
by everything you've thought.

Magic Marker Blue and First Name

Ornithology invites obsessing on the open windows, which are really squares assigned a function. Segregating choice from an *as though*. There are remunerative sanctions placed by heart on people like adhesive name tags that say "HI!" and leave a space for magic marker blue and a first name. See how important nomenclature runs in narrative balloon payments that sign the sky. It's mirth that clumps of people inadvertently achieve. In rooms too white for earth to seem at home. The gravity imposed is from the brain's directly pointing to agreed-upon denominations of a pasture. Worth holds still. Fits nicely into snapshots. These excuses to have come together. Held at arm's length saturating possibilities of consciousness. If you can name that pair of wings, you'll win a metonymic prize. Two eyes distinctly chaperoning fragrances surmised.

Scale Model of a Spirit Wall

The safest arrow to respect is one-way. Live or nubile, we
effect the lunar probabilities with a subtle thunder. Thumbs
seem poised. The neighbors chat about configurations when
we say *entonces*. People wait for something more. Until the
lowest profile falls for air time as prevailing myth. The only
host we know is brazen with these kickbacks that equate to a
cement. Why don't we hypothesize an anger that will steam
wallpaper from . . . a retrospective lasso for a conscience?
A license to be working hard. Pituitary nonsense capable
of being tamed again entraps the guts. Maims lurking daisies
if you say narration's to be stricken from our affluence.
Demeanor is a favor to bestow upon the soulful diametric
pose all winter. Do me the favor of remaining as you
are. Positioned thus from the voluptuous blue-seeming
mountain. Yards apart from the incinerative soul.

Tools Tired of Being Humid

Pax began the wording of the drug. A muscle that's supposed to hold my knee in place has gone out on its own, *needs to be touched.* Though solitude costs firm and crippling bucks *not for me to say.* Obligatory feathers of hello cross skin for comfort, shadow buyers needing (must we add) to be ecstaticized. *Voila* the world's own window. Strawberry patch or pippin orch-. Computer space. The leisure we accumulate won't transfer to an elder's bake sale with the proceeds gone to clarity. The lump of each that's physical is led into a place and handed for a while then visits home. As any stranger taking care without the tension that surrounds the small imprisonment of these relationships. Tools tired of being humid ask themselves to dry their good steel over water onto rough-toned wood. She's come to sell things with her rhetoric that isn't slow. It's sudsy as a low-field wash. It's vined as legs are numb in frames crisp that match the antiques in this house.

Her Docile Art

On approach, her docile art collects on consequence.
Grows into circumstantial lore. Define for me *begging
the question*. She was a sure-fire ophthalmologist who now
looks at her watch for scheduled meals, spools her way to
the broad waiting area in front of closed doors of the dining
room. Whatever's served for lunch is small in cottage
cheese-sized bowls. A confusion factor hankers to be seen,
is shirked out of the photograph. She pulls off freeze-dried
stamens. Issues orders to her offspring on the phone.
Buys liquor, home delivery. She chills the score, derives a
huge sum from the witness stand of the uneducated she
has framed. Derivative angst sounds persuasive to the
unprepared. No job deserves the girth that it presumes.
What has declared itself to be affordable is actually already
true and seeking to be called reality.

What Better Trunkline

These mile-tipped paintings recommend themselves
freehand to fossil donors who appoint themselves to
blue derogatories. When is skin a subset of mobility?
This lamp to touch a body heat interned. Small flocking
bunched against the carpet. Sourced in a spectator's wants.
The dialogue's omission pounces from a firm position of
regret. Platters silver soak time. Pews with givers seated in
thrall at a regression to the mean re: forgiveness. What plex
leads us through the campground noise, what better
trunkline, what autonomy for birth? The usefulness flies
home and calls another for gratuity. A scolding voice forms
the elastic side of caring. Junctures pass quite ably centime-
ters. Keen on being swerved past. In the same sentence as
forgetfulness is the misnomer *mental health*. What was the
name my father missed? The name my father always
washed? Debriefing the dementia. Skin betters drain matter
of course from mythical end-of-the-line.

She's So Specific

Constructure helps apply the paint on income and on
lack. Welcome to *Anyberg*. Creosote spans walkways and
comportment. Dizzy byways left-of-center nurture keep.
I write in someone else's house. The atmosphere has
nothing frail. A pendulum so left wing that I keep *not
faltering*. Is this the eddy you would want? Why nature in
the designated pocket? Foremost, I'm uncomfortable here
and elsewhere. She asks my advice then surls. I say *you
asked*. I am given to inquire where we are going to eat
mantra. Where practice? Where faint? Where are we
going to teach yoga? Or when are we not going to carouse?
Don't look to me for discipline. I weevil and I mime.
I pour direct address into the air stripped from the avenues.
She's so specific about her wants I almost understand her.

Thursday About 3:32

One of the niche markets is a socket strained through pulp.
The sky server keeps coming around to sell us what we've
bought *inclusive evidence*. The shuttle between piecemeal
efforts and these souvenirs fresh from catalpa. Much of
amelioration chives in brackets hurtled by the river shore.
A man is clogging up the aisle, oblivious to girth more
obstacle than treat. Tell me a story about damsels and repeat
screams. Tell me present tense is curly. Sacrifice what little
seems affordable by moving off the chemlab portion of our
show. *What're you doing, say, Thursday at about 3:32?* Guts
frequently spill wide-open fetes. How do you take money
and transform it into feasting with the lollygags? Notice
people don't dress up on planes. Cash flow suspends the
citrus open flower. *See what I'm saying* protects him from
ace in the hole mentality. Respect is an old-fashioned thing.
Resisting leapfrog habits over Chinese herbs.

Hand In Hand

Breeding when little else to do. You add this template to a
laminated bedside manner that surpasses no manner at all.
Is it fair to say that thermal underwear trespasses on the
body's nakedness? Her goal's *you in a box* in keeping with
her narrow definition. Being in love has bonus points from
which to reel. Breathing's not very hard not very often
slightly warm to touch. Found satisfied, found able to be
washed. A little risen lady. Fresh, warm bread. The fact of
watching corresponds with each admittance. Take good
notes. Avenge or something painted angels. There's a type
of wind that's mainly narrative. The chakras learning
English like fall-of-Saigon. Immense deep feeling and a
future without temperature.

A Burden and No More

Say you (at 29,000 feet) keep a secret once it no longer is a
secret. Your host rises early and you miss the leverage of a
pale pill. Keepsakes hover on the off-rink likely one more
than the angel thought. Late brunch past altitude. The
feather in our grasp this sudden and this winded longitude.
Perimeters require attention span. Log many hours of fright
time. In a frame whose contents soak through careful study
over time and space. Altimeters have wined and dined their
charges as uncomfortably as I have listened sans recording
impulse to the hum. The jigger of a proxy fight. The cut the
crew receives. The living well that comes with overly
projecting onto persons, numbs these sensitivities. What
people do to get a buck. Generic promise and politeness.
Chums write back and false alarms do not. Stool pigeons
face a different death from loved ones. What price safety?
Husbands quite unloved for whom their charges are a
burden and no more within these stagnant and unstylish
frames.

Short Silver

I really think I do not want to sleep with him (again).
And as the man seemed dumb by sound, I found he was
(intelligent). Some purse strings, seraphim and such white
sheet rock. Semblances must matter twice (triumphant).
The genius violinist I can't name had fingers George would
die for and already owned. Pagannini strongly linked to
Luce. Sewn madras box of figs. Soroptimist laments still
sweet when we are under this duress and such? The Cayman
Islands plush themselves into my postcard window. Write
carefully to write well toward overstock. A yelpless slow
interior, gliding downhill. The cement of it still far from
softening temerity.

Fixed mind also fluid mind, a woman in the throes of
(l)earning harmony

Brakes On

How is anything we love a non-emergency? What I lack now
is a shift teeming with classified estrangement. Simulacra
decrease the imagination some. The attention of attention,
or a *bought* department of dis-justice. Events where several
get stuck. Brakes on the stern father. Skeptical press has
leverage used and new. Arrange to simplify a system of left
turns. *Clear need not be cold.* A jungle gym of mind astride
the body. Homelessness, therefore, a critical caboose.
Investment of enormous wealth. People listen in their
accents. Delivery, distinct from deliver us, deliverance.
Support being equal to (all other things) the lobby
ratcheting a sealed row of beads to pluck or savor or arrest.
Is talking a sport? Which musical instrument do you play
in my spare time? Fast speaking may connote a differential
in the speed of thought and voice, induced by stuttering.
Attention's the result. Along the street. A pecking order
faltering.

Within the Standard Dissonance

The key to cleaning up is line of sight within the standard
dissonance and pipeline. *Are we there yet?* Follicles outnum-
ber nurturants. Make me an adjective that I can innuendo.
Threatened evidence near wing-tipped shoes. Capstone
lighthouse feasance. Orange blossoms melt the depths near
lumber's woodland breach of conscience. Peak lessons in
hair part stress the impetus. The pen rehearses breaking ties.
White lies. Amour is how you whittle what you do. Clean
clothes include darned socks. Salt pork, B vitamins, the
probability of long life. Sanctions plague us. Dominate the
market swiftly open in its tracks. The open stacks, a learned
encroachment spilling a sworn fabrication.

The Pink

Recovery is not a sport. And values need not be religious.
Leverage sequencing and boisterous light just bathing in
autonomy. Cooperation pokes its nose into a structured
wilderness. The thought of being interested in forth before
the back. A campus. *Compus mentus*. Shadow is a chore.
The goal is looking through a porthole so the consequence
might be a florid chant. Let's let it go. Let's meld the color
pink with something in the sun. A painted wash. Release,
suppress, delineate the pluses and the cons. How do you get
famous if you grow? Commandments spawn an icing of self
evidence. Round corners, blend the lead excaliber retrieval.
Pack a pair of shorts. Where there will palsy any number of
erosions. Adjectives especially feel wholly and prismatic
blue. Having learned the taste of sure affection. Having
learned the ways of learning you.

Traffic

Free will trespasses on Sonoran things. Connective quality
of fall. The desert paint unseen. A league once limber
changing cartilage. The cloth and sibilants confuse perpetu-
ally cinch points. Clatter, bandages, full parts of speech.
As buckets of ideas drift through conversation. Fascia board
in brown is chipping legacy atop these just-constructed
columns. Sophistication comes in thimbles and is hoarded.
Would a tank of fish be good if we just paused and looked?
Compassion moves out of the way, almost unseen. The
faculty of reason squelches an excuse to step away. One
shot of wheat grass, equaling two pounds of vegetables
not consumed. Hitched to the inevitable monkey work
of getting to your destination. The confessional's entirely
full of a town meeting emphasizing strategy. With bodies
in form, yield far ahead of what it costs.

Gesture and wake, first slender path accompanied breadth

Labor Intensity

Catch me mid-fluency: remind of paths these shoes have
crossed. I ride the bus one morning, shine leakage from the
camera to canvas. *You who represent your town.* The whirring
of recorder. As full freedom rinses sectors from this place
point. Stake in the duration ground. *As I was saying*, proffer,
league, and leisure mount campaigns. We are a softness.
Thereby parallelograms won't release inklings of hetero-
versus same in brief. Long nearly extrapolates the seared
impeachment birch. *Sign here* and go away. The rapture
follows easily our thirst. Ten times its weight in evidence.
Frothing element's quiescent patch of snow. Trace what
you remember wedged between repeat signs about to
self-destruct. I have the script right here marked *yours*.

Latitude hand over hand near long neck, forces well outside
our control spanning the water

Sectional

Come lie down with the ideas that redeem me. Come
rehearse release from lamentation. Soon elders a brothel
coat of blue where red would be. There is a claim form
somewhere half-completed. Playoffs are impending.
Come lie down with minds lodged here. Come hold your
temper quiet in the clutches of my invitation. Come revere
deciduous placation. Torque was only the beginning of this
water. Framed once or situated where a nest would envy
borders. Langostino in our midst was memoried past water.
Taste salt and disappear from hinge to any mythic grief.

No straight line in nature, hearing all the same

In Vitro Ponce

A situation enmities itself in time in tune in vitro ponce as though we liked our fraying happiness. Posture wheels itself to funerals until the cancellation notice is found taped to window panes. *What happened* flowed from every pair of lips prepared to quiver on the right side of the doctor's breast. Impractical regrets were shared by several warm-blooded . . . Zoos emptied of contentment had been thought infected. Silly putty prose dug heels into the washday with its sleek new ostinati pure as minted breath to carry off unfree as human beings on payrolls. The meeting schedule interfered with routine walks along wide slabs of pavement pretty lah-de-dah as far as fat goes in the tax domain. The market bore resemblance to a dawdle-proof dimension of unholiness. The meantime shoved the world into a quarter nelson and reclined through the economy full stop along three levels of ascension.

Pertinence, full dish of silver, lap dogs lapping what's familiar

Take A Number

Production (keep in mind) is all we have in common. All
we hold. The formula's *fail to engage* to yield the gift of
separation. *Really is a gift* when you can learn. To have held
still. Attention as great gift. Of patterned giving. (Take a
number.) Mimes come in (several flavors) handy. All the
world's a gift of *target audience* along the spectrum audible
to practically inaudible. *Do not* get buried under. *Do not*
immerse yourself in tiny things. *Do not* metonym the
whole fish for the tingly little gills that flash their form of
acquiescence. *Do not* take lessons in an enterprise you do
not mean to swallow. Save perspective with attention as
prerequisite for your true and only love (comes first).
Boughs tend to break. And who's your baby willing to be
now, with wind so close impending as an episode to drive
over known tundra.

Sheila E. Murphy lives in Phoenix, Arizona. She is a widely
published poet who has performed her work internationally.
In 1999, Murphy was the guest of the Brisbane Writers
Festival in Queensland Australia. She read the following year
in England as part of a residency in Devon for the Arvon
Foundation, where she collaborated with poet/painter Rupert
Loydell in facilitating a weeklong workshop. In 2000,
Murphy read at the Boston Poetry Festival and for the Lit
City Series in New Orleans. Murphy publishes widely in
literary magazines and writes prolifically, in many different
styles. Prose poems, including what she terms "American
haibun," are among her favorite styles. Since 1999, Murphy
has also been engaged in creating visual work, using both
digital and physical formats, some of them including text.
Her published work is archived at The Ohio State University
Libraries, Rare Books and Manuscripts, as part of the Avant
Collection established by Dr. John M. Bennett.

OTHER BOOKS BY PLEASURE BOAT STUDIO: A LITERARY PRESS

Schilling, from a Study in Lost Time. Terrell Guillory
    ISBN 1-939355-09-2, $16.95, 156 pages, fiction
Rumours: A Memoir of a British POW in WWII, Chas Mayhead
    ISBN 1-929355-06-8, $17.95, 201 pages, nonfiction
The Immigrant's Table, Mary Lou Sanelli
    ISBN 1-929355-15-7, $13.95, poetry
The Enduring Vision of Norman Mailer, Barry H. Leeds
    ISBN 1-929355-11-4, $18, literary criticism
Women in the Garden, Mary Lou Sanelli
    ISBN 1-929355-14-9, $13.95, poetry
Pronoun Music, Richard Cohen
    ISBN1-929355-03-3, $16, short stories
If You Were With Me Everything Would Be All Right, Ken Harvey
    ISBN 1-929355-02-5, $16, short stories
The 8th Day of the Week, Al Kessler
    ISBN 1-929355-00-9, $16, fiction
Another Life, and Other Stories, Edwin Weihe
    ISBN 1-929355-011-7, $16, short stories
Saying the Necessary, Edward Harkness
    ISBN 0-9651413-7-3 (hard), $22; 0-9651413-9-X (paper), $14, poetry
Nature Lovers, Charles Potts
    ISBN 1-929355-04-1, $10, poetry
In Memory of Hawks, & Other Stories from Alaska, Irving Warner
    ISBN 0-9651413-4-9, $15, 210 pages, fiction
The Politics of My Heart, William Slaughter
    ISBN 0-9651413-0-6, $12.95, 96 pages, poetry
The Rape Poems, Frances Driscoll
    ISBN 0-9651413-1-4, $12.95, 88 pages, poetry
When History Enters the House: Essays from Central Europe,
Michael Blumenthal
    ISBN 0-9651413-2-2, $15, 248 pages, nonfiction
Setting Out: The Education of Li-li, Tung Nien,
Translated from the Chinese by Mike O'Connor
    ISBN 0-9651413-3-0, $15, 160 pages, fiction

Our Chapbook Series:

No. 1: The Handful of Seeds: Three and a Half Essays,
Andrew Schelling
    ISBN 0-9651413-5-7, $7, 36 pages, nonfiction
No. 2: Original Sin, Michael Daley
    ISBN 0-9651413-6-5, $8, 36 pages, poetry
No. 3: Too Small to Hold You, Kate Reavey
    ISBN 1-929355-05-x, $8, poetry
No. 4: The Light on Our Faces: A Therapy Dialogue,
Lee Miriam Whitman-Raymond
    ISBN 1-929355-12-2, $8, 36 pages, poetry
No 5: Eye, William Bridges
    ISBN 1-929355-13-0, $8, 20 pages, poetry
No.6: The Work of Maria Rainer Rilke: Selected "New Poems"
Translated by Alice Derry
    ISBN 1-929355-10-6, $10, 44 pages, poetry

From Our Backlist (in limited editions):

Desire, Jody Aliesan
    ISBN 0-912887-11-7, $14, poetry (an Empty Bowl book)
Dreams of the Hand, Susan Goldwitz
    ISBN 0-912887-12-5, $14, poetry (an Empty Bowl book)
Lineage, Mary Lou Sanelli
    No ISBN, $14, poetry (an Empty Bowl book)
P'u Ming's Oxherding Tales, Red Pine
    No ISBN, $10, Trans from Chinese with Illustrations, fiction
                (an Empty Bowl book)
The Basin: Poems from a Chinese Province, Mike O'Connor
    ISBN 0-912887-20-6, $10/$20, (paper/ hardbound), Poetry
                (an Empty Bowl book)
The Straits, Michael Daley
    ISBN 0-912887-04-4, $10, poetry (an Empty Bowl book)
In Our Hearts and Minds: The Northwest and Central America,
    Ed. Michael Daley, ISBN 0-912887-18-4, $12, poetry and prose
                (an Empty Bowl book)

The Rainshadow, Mike O'Connor
No ISBN, $16, poetry (an Empty Bowl book)
Untold Stories, William Slaughter
ISBN 1-91288724-9, $10/$20, (paper/hardbound), poetry
(an Empty Bowl book)
In Blue Mountain Dusk, Tim McNulty
ISBN 0-9651413-8-1, $12.95, poetry (a Broken Moon book)

ORDERS:

Most Pleasure Boat Studio books
are available directly from PBS
or through any of the following:
SPD—Tel: 800-869-7553, Fax 510-524-0852
Partners/West—Tel: 425-227-8486, Fax: 425-204-2448
Baker & Taylor—Tel: 800-775-1100, Fax: 800-775-7480
Ingram—Tel: 615-793-5000, Fax: 615-287-5429
Amazon.com
Barnesandnoble.com

for PBS orders:
Tel/Fax: 888-810-5308
Email: pleasboat@nyc.rr.com
Website: www.pbstudio.com

How We Got Our Name:

from *Pleasure Boat Studio,*
an essay written by Ouyang Xiu,
Song Dynasty poet, essayist, and scholar
(January 25, 1043)

"If one is not anxious for profit, even at the risk of danger, or is not convicted of a crime and forced to embark; rather, if one has a favorable breeze and gentle seas and is able to rest comfortably on a pillow and mat, sailing several hundred miles in a single day, then is boat travel not enjoyable? Of course, I have no time for such diversions. But since 'pleasure boat' is the designation of boats used for such pastimes, I have now adopted it as the name of my studio. Is there anything wrong with that?"

Translated by Ronald Egan